The Chameleon

Text by Claudia Schnieper

The Chameleon

Translated by Noel Simon

Photographs by Max Meier

J.M. Dent & Sons Ltd
London

First published in Great Britain 1989
English translation © J.M. Dent & Sons Ltd 1989
Originally published in German under the title
Das Chamäleon – Meisterschütze und Verwandlungskünstler
© 1986 by Kinderbuchverlag KBV Luzern AG

Printed in Germany
This book is set in 14/16½pt Linotron Century Schoolbook
by Gee Graphics Ltd, Crayford, Kent
for J.M. Dent & Sons Ltd
91 Clapham High Street,
London SW4

British Library Cataloguing in Publication Data
Schnieper, Claudia
    The chameleon.
    1. Chameleons
    I. Title II. Meier, Max III. Das Chamaleon. English
    597.95

ISBN 0-460-07040-I

The chameleon is an extraordinary animal. It looks like a miniature fairy-tale dragon, with eyes mounted in turrets that can move independently of each other. While one remains fixed attentively on us the other jerkily examines a fly. It can suddenly change colour, becoming green, brown, red, blue, yellow, violet, white, or black, even spotted and striped. The slow and very deliberate steps it takes when stalking its prey are in marked contrast with the way, swift as an arrow, it captures its prey with its immensely long tongue.

Chameleons evolved from a group of huge primeval lizards which lived in the age of the dinosaurs. Their present-day descendants have been on earth for about 100 million years, and in all that time have hardly changed at all.

Together with their nearest relatives the lizards, chameleons belong to the group of animals known as reptiles, which includes the tortoises and turtles as well as the crocodiles and snakes. Many people imagine that all reptiles crawl on their bellies, but that is not so: some walk in a perfectly normal manner.

Chameleons live in tropical and subtropical regions, mainly in Africa and on the island of Madagascar in the Indian Ocean. In some countries they are worshipped by the local people who believe they bring good luck; in others the people are terrified of these harmless insect-eaters. The ancient Greek name for chameleon was 'earth lion', probably a derogatory term, for the little animal is anything but lion-like. If threatened it simply drops off its perch and falls to the ground.

The chameleon family is divided into two separate branches: the common chameleons, of which at least eighty species are known – about half of them found only in Madagascar – and the stump-tailed chameleons with about sixteen species, distinguished by a short tail and occurring in West and East Africa and Madagascar. Like all reptiles, chameleons are said to be cold-blooded. Their body heat depends on the temperature of their surroundings, which is why they live in warm climates. Cold has a crippling effect on reptiles, and they die if the temperature drops below freezing for any length of time.

The chameleons include both giant and pygmy varieties. The largest is Oustalet's chameleon from Madagascar, which can grow up to a length of 63 cm, in contrast with the smallest stump-tailed chameleon which measures only 4 cm.

Households in southern Spain have long kept chameleons as living fly catchers. Their long tongues constantly shoot out at lightning speed to catch flies, gnats and other insect pests. Children are often very fond of these little 'dragons', carrying them around on their shoulders or walking about with them clinging firmly to their wrists.

The European (or common) chameleon is now almost extinct in southern Spain. Most of its habitat has been destroyed. Almost the entire coastal belt in which it once lived has been cleared and the countryside taken over by sprawling colonies of holiday homes. The European chameleon is 25-30 cm long, has a slightly serrated ridge along its back, and a triangular 'helmet' on the back of its head. Like all chameleons it is adapted to living in trees and bushes. Its claw-like feet are designed for firmly grasping branches and twigs, its long prehensile tail providing extra support. It is particularly fond, as here, of lying in wait on the almost leafless tamarisk trees growing along the coast, on the look-out for prey. Its diet of insects and spiders is supplemented by plant food and mineral-rich soil. The common chameleon is also found in Greece, Arabia, Asia, India and Sri Lanka. This slow-moving animal is astonishingly adaptable: in the desert it digs itself a hole in which it lives as protection against the fierce heat of the day and the surprisingly cold nights.

This photograph shows a four-horned chameleon in the full splendour of its display colouring. Within seconds it can once again become dull. How does the animal manage to do it? We, too, can change the colour of our skin. When we are frightened we go either pale or red, as we do when we lose our temper or are embarrassed. Changes of mood affect chameleons in exactly the same way, but their skin language is much more pronounced. Not only are anger and fear obvious from a distance, their skin colour is influenced by heat, sunshine, cold and darkness. When they are courting or sick they also change colour. The chameleon's body is covered with scales of different sizes and shapes. If you look closely, you can distinguish round, oval, serrated or angular scales. With impressive horns and throat sac puffed up to its full extent, this male threatens his enemy. Including his outstretched tail, this chameleon is 35 cm long.

Of all this animal's many fascinating features, the most extraordinary is its eyes. The enormous eye balls bulge like domes. The eyelids close to form a ring at the centre, leaving only a tiny opening for the pupil. A chameleon's eyes are able to operate independently of each other and to look in different directions: keeping one eye on a crab on the ground, for example, while the other watches a predatory bird in the sky. It can also focus on an object with both eyes for, like us, chameleons have 'binocular' vision,

that is to say they can use both eyes together. This enables them to estimate distance with remarkable accuracy. When the chameleon gets within range of its prey it turns its head towards it, measuring the distance with its eyes. A moment later its tongue shoots out. It hardly ever misses; its equipment functions perfectly.

The flap-necked chameleon (above) shows not only its eye-acrobatics; it also displays tiny teeth, attached to the edges of the upper and lower jaws.

The chameleon's feet clamp themselves firmly around twigs and small branches: they are not suited to walking on smooth, flat surfaces. The forefeet are arranged in such a way that two toes joined together face inwards and three outwards. The arrangement of the hindfeet is the other way round: three toes face inwards and two outwards. These 'opposable' toes form a pincer grip for grasping twigs and branches; they can also be used for digging. The prehensile tail serves as an extra limb by curling around branches and anchoring the animal firmly. The flap-necked chameleon on the right even hangs by its tail like a trapeze artist. When either asleep or exposed to the sun the tail is coiled up in a neat spiral. The male mountain chameleon in the upper picture on page 13 sleeps peacefully.

The basilisk chameleon (above) walks with stiff legs and extended tail to the security of the nearest bush, but all the time its eyes are constantly scanning its surroundings.

Chameleons have no visible ears: in any event their hearing is of only minor importance as they rely mainly on their eyesight for defence.

When pursuing its prey the chameleon's slow and deliberate movements are in marked contrast with the lightning speed at which its catching apparatus, the tongue, functions. Learning to survive calls for quite a lot of experience. Chameleons seldom live long in captivity, mainly because they are not properly fed. It is almost impossible to provide the many different kinds of insects that they need. This explains why most zoos have given up trying to exhibit this animal.

The chameleon's tongue is a remarkable instrument. It can be at least as long as the animal itself. But how does it function, and how does the animal stow away its enormous tongue in its mouth? Imagine the tongue as a long, slender, finely-folded concertina. Extremely elastic muscles, attached to the throat and running the length of the lower jaw, pull the tongue backwards and forwards. At the back of the jaw is a special bone – the hyoid bone – with its own set of powerful muscles which help to catapult the tongue forward. The tip of the tongue is thickened into a club shape, rather like the tip of an elephant's trunk.

16

Let us see how this crack shot actually shoots. First it fixes its prey with its eyes. Then its tongue is brought into action. Its mouth opens and the tongue, wound up like a spring, is catapulted forward. It stretches itself lengthwise like a rubber band. This happens so quickly that the human eye finds it almost impossible to follow: it takes only a fraction of a second to strike. Curling the sticky tip of its tongue around its victim, the chameleon draws it slowly into its mouth. Though it struggles with all its might the insect has no chance of escape. The tip of the chameleon's tongue acts like a suction pad, and once it has caught something does not let go. This grasshopper is first crunched between strong jaws before being chewed. Large chameleons can even catch small mice, lizards, or birds.

Chameleons are not the only animals to change the colour of their skin. Many other reptiles, as well as frogs and fish, can do so too. These changes are controlled by the nervous system, the brain giving the nerves the 'order' which stimulates the colour cells to change.

The outermost layer of skin is paper-thin and colourless and made out of horny material. The lower layers of skin – the hypodermis – contains a variety of colour cells lying close to each other. They contain pigments, both coloured and colourless. As the colour cells alter in size the pigments either concentrate or disperse, in the process changing both the colour and the pattern of the skin. This explains why an animal can change from one colour to another for no obvious reason. It has also been discovered that camouflage plays a less important role than might be imagined, and often happens quite by

chance. A green chameleon placed on a yellow leaf may remain just as green as it was. At night, chameleons are usually light coloured and thus more conspicuous than they need be. The graceful chameleon (above) protects itself from the sun's rays by assuming a lighter colour.

Light colours throw the radiation back, reflecting it. Dark colours, on the other hand, absorb the heat better. The chameleon on the left-hand page lives on Mount Kenya up to a height of 3000 meters, where it has to endure cold rain, hail and low temperatures.

Mount Cameroun lies in the humid tropics of West Africa, not far from the sea. This is where the mountain chameleon lives. It is found in the rain forest at a height of 600 to 1200 meters, living in the dense undergrowth beneath gigantic trees – the picture shows some of the huge tree ferns which grow in this region. The mountain chameleon is well camouflaged, and its best protection from hungry birds and snakes, which are quick to spot any movement, is to remain absolutely still. But it has no defence against its most deadly enemy: man. The local people clear large areas of the rain forest in order to grow crops, thus destroying the chameleon's habitat. The quickest and easiest way of clearing forest and bush is to burn it, and this is commonly done on a large scale. Conservationists are doing all they can to protect the tropical rain forest and prevent this green paradise from being transformed into a desolate wasteland.

Above is a female mountain chameleon in her sleeping place. She leaves her sleeping place to warm herself by basking in the sun. She will then move to a favourite spot to lie in wait for prey to come within reach of her tongue. She obtains water by licking the dew from leaves.

Only a short distance from the female mountain chameleon sits a male. With his pair of long, ringed horns, the prominent ridge along his back and large tail-crest, he is an impressive sight. He wants to mate with the female, and has ornamented himself with the most wonderful sky-blue markings. The chameleon is not a sociable animal, and will fiercely defend its territory against intruders of its own kind. The only time chameleons are forced to abandon their solitary way of life is when they wish to pair off for breeding. A female is usually courted by more than one male, and this often leads to bitter fighting. When rival males confront one another (three pictures on the right) they make it clear whether or not they are in fighting mood. One male threatens his opponent by opening his mouth as wide as possible, hissing furiously, and becoming a light colour. He stands sideways on so that he appears larger and more intimidating

than from the front. At the same time he expands his body and raises it high in the air. When he inflates his brightly coloured throat he looks even more menacing. His rival nevertheless refuses to be driven off – the matter can only be settled in close combat. The two males snap and bite – sometimes until blood flows – and try to stab each other with their horns. The weaker (on the right) goes a darker colour. Had he been decisively beaten he would have toppled off the branch and hung from its underside. It is normal practice for chameleons to make themselves less conspicuous by hiding either behind or under branches. Rocking gently back and forth is another trick of concealment. The chameleon is then easily mistaken for one of many wind-blown leaves.

In the picture on the left a male flap-necked chameleon gazes at a female. This species derives its name from the two lobes – flaps of skin – on the back of the head which – like the ears of an elephant – can be erected when the animal is excited. The female (above right) evidently likes the suitor, as her green colouring shows. The male climbs towards her and tries to mount. When the female is ready to mate she signifies submission by changing from green to brown.

The age at which chameleons can bear young differs from one species to another. Food and climate play an important part. Some species are mature by the age of nine months, others later. Chameleons have no firm mating season. After they have mated the females are able to store sperm in their bodies for long periods, until conditions are favourable, a process known as 'delayed implantation'.

Male chameleons, like lizards and snakes, possess a special reproductive organ, the 'hemipenis'. Males, which otherwise can hardly be distinguished from females, can be recognized by the swollen pouches at the root of the tail, in which the pair of hemipenes is housed, and which turn outward during mating. Only one is used at each mating. Chameleons mate repeatedly over a period of days. Throughout this time these normally solitary animals remain close to each other. Sooner or later the eggs in the female's belly are fertilized by the male semen and she becomes pregnant. From now on she will repel any suitors who approach her. Her threat colour is indeed unmistakeable, but when a male fails to be deterred even by such obvious signs the female hisses furiously, rocks her body to and fro, and tries to bite.

Despite having blown himself up fully, the male in the bottom right-hand picture is taking no chances and draws back.

When females show by
their colour that they are
pregnant, the males keep
at a respectful distance.
This body language is
understood by all and
does not need to be
learned, for it is
instinctive.

The fertilized egg cells develop in the female's belly until they become eggs. The length of the gestation period is dependent upon climatic conditions and the availability of food. Shortly before laying her eggs, the female becomes so swollen that she can scarcely eat as there is no longer room in her stomach for food. She moves awkwardly and even more slowly than usual. When ready to lay she climbs down to the ground and digs a hole in the soil. In it she lays one egg after another – anywhere from 30 to 130 altogether. By the time she has finished laying, this flap-necked chameleon weighs only half as much as before! She then covers the eggs with soil. After that the female pays no further attention to her nest. She is very weak and it is important that during the coming days she should eat well to restore her strength.

The embryos start to develop. The moist, warm soil prevents the eggs from becoming either too dry or too cold. Growing embryos require plenty of nourishment: egg-yolk and white of egg provide them with all their needs. Each embryo is surrounded by a membrane containing the amniotic fluid in which it develops. In order that this tiny organism can 'breathe' in its egg it is connected to a 'bladder', which serves the double purpose of lung and waste-disposal bag.

The warmer the soil the more quickly the embryos grow in the eggs and the stronger they will be. After seven months and ten days the big moment has arrived: beneath the loose soil there is gentle movement. A tiny head first appears. Then a glistening wet creature crawls to the surface. It is about 4 cm long and weighs 3 grams, but already looks like a full-grown chameleon. One baby chameleon after another climbs out of the ground and stands blinking at the bright sunlight through closed eyes. This particular nest produced fifty-two. Not all the embryos survive: the eggs are delicate. Too much heat or cold can kill them, as can bacterial or viral infection; or they may be eaten or trampled by animals.

many animals would spot and attack them. The young are not even safe from their own kind. The newborn chameleons at once start looking for small insects to catch. To start with hunting is unquestionably difficult: they are not yet crack shots, and their first attempts often miss. But as a growing chameleon needs plenty of food, they get in a lot of practice. The young chameleon in the upper picture is drinking a drop of water.

Young chameleons are as unsociable as their elders. They soon establish their own territories, in the process fighting among themselves, as in the right-hand picture. The little one in the lower left-hand picture has already been stopped by the bigger one: the loser hangs from the underside of the branch and turns a dark colour. The victor arrogantly displays his green garb.

From the moment of birth young chameleons have to fend for themselves. They must be quick and agile in leaving the egg. Slowness would be disastrous as

Chameleons, lizards and snakes have a tough skin which is nowhere near as elastic as ours. It encloses the body like a coat of chain mail. As scaly animals grow their skin becomes too tight for them. Until they are fully grown they must shed their skin at regular intervals.

The flap-necked chameleon in the upper left-hand picture sits motionless on a branch. Its skin is dull and pale and looks taught. This is what chameleons look like when they are about to moult. The outer skin suddenly bursts open and hangs from the body in tatters.

In dry and sunny weather the process is quicker than when conditions are cold and damp. Using its feet, the chameleon helps pull off the old skin. Underneath, it has already grown a new and slightly larger skin. Its new coat glows in fresh, bright colours.

Animals often adapt in fantastic ways to their surroundings, as you can see on the following two pages. Most chameleons lay eggs, burying them in the ground and leaving them for the sun to hatch. But there are some species living in cold mountain climates whose eggs would freeze if they were laid in the soil. After they have been fertilized the female therefore keeps them safe and warm in her body until they are fully developed. Animals giving birth to live young are called viviparous. One of them, Jackson's chameleon, lives in the highlands of East Africa up to a height of 3000 meters. The male is about 30 cm long and carries three imposing ringed horns on its forehead; the female's horns are usually so much smaller as to be only just visible. After mating (picture page 34, left) the embryos start to develop in the normal way. The female can carry up to forty in her belly; by the time she is ready to give birth she is as round as a barrel.

While giving birth the female clings to a branch. One young after another pours forth, still surrounded by the translucent egg membrane which sticks to a branch or leaf. A few fall to the ground, but that doesn't matter – newborn chameleons are as light as thistledown and have supple bones. The outer wrapping has already split open; the newborn young wriggles head foremost out of the membrane, in which the remains of the yolk can still be seen. It measures about 4 cm and is already a competent climber. It quickly climbs up the branch towards the sunlight. As with chameleons hatched from eggs underground, it is self-sufficient from its first moment.

The mother takes no further interest in her offspring. She has given birth to eighteen young. Having freed themselves from the membrane in which they were born, they have all started to hunt small insects. Their tiny horns can be clearly seen on their muzzles and above their eyes.

All animals have their own language by which they can communicate with others of their kind. Chameleons nod or shake their head, rock and sway on the branch on which they are perching, and open their mouths and hiss. Crests, back ridge, or horns give each particular species a distinctive appearance.

These are not simply ornaments or weapons but also the means by which chameleons convey information. From their expressive colour language we can understand how sensitive these small creatures are. It seems as if the chameleon's ability to change colour helps compensate for its inability to move as quickly as other animals. To take a particular species, the flap-necked chameleon, as an example, you can see how this animal indicates its mood by different colours and patterns.

In the top left-hand picture a female threatens with open mouth and inflated throat. Her yellow stripes are designed to scare away strange animals or even other chameleons.

The dark orange- and green-spotted coat of the female at lower left is a signal that she wants to have nothing to do with males as she is pregnant. In comparison with her, the female above right appears meek and nervous. She has lost a fight and has gone 'black with anger'. The male (below) is pale and conspicuous. He is aggressively wooing a female and is determined to be noticed. He displays his head flaps and inflates his throat, which has the effect of making him appear larger and more impressive.

Can you see the chameleon in the picture on the left? Among the brown undergrowth of the rain forest it is perfectly camouflaged, looking like a dry leaf: hence its name 'leaf chameleon'. The short, thick tail is the identification mark of the stump-tailed chameleons, of which there are about sixteen species forming their own separate branch of the chameleon family. Stump-tailed chameleons live mostly on low bushes or among decaying wood on the forest floor. They are less brightly coloured than other chameleons. Little is known about their habits. Their colouring blends so well with their surroundings that they are practically invisible.

This colourful female chameleon lives in the mountain rain forests of Cameroun in West Africa. 'Earth lioness' seems an appropriate name for this little animal. She makes it absolutely clear that she does not enjoy being photographed.

Chameleons are an example of how inventive nature can be. Some animals resort to the most ingenious means of survival. By using a variety of colours and unusual patterns, together with extremely slow and deliberate movements, chameleons avoid drawing attention upon themselves. At the right moment they strike their prey at lightning speed. Their moods and feelings are clearly shown by changes of colour – but at present we understand only a little of the chameleon's complex body language.